I Love Sports

Volleyball

by Erica Donner

Bullfrog Books

Ideas for Parents and Teachers

Bullfrog Books let children practice reading informational text at the earliest reading levels. Repetition, familiar words, and photo labels support early readers.

Before Reading

- Discuss the cover photo. What does it tell them?
- Look at the picture glossary together. Read and discuss the words.

Read the Book

- "Walk" through the book and look at the photos. Let the child ask questions. Point out the photo labels.
- Read the book to the child, or have him or her read independently.

After Reading

- Prompt the child to think more. Ask: Have you ever played volleyball? Were you on an indoor court or did you play at the beach?

Bullfrog Books are published by Jump!
5357 Penn Avenue South
Minneapolis, MN 55419
www.jumplibrary.com

Library of Congress Cataloging-in-Publication Data

Names: Donner, Erica, author.
Title: Volleyball / by Erica Donner.
Description: Minneapolis, Minnesota: Jump!, Inc.
[2017] | Series: I love sports | Includes index.
Identifiers: LCCN 2016007178 (print)
LCCN 2016007543 (ebook)
ISBN 9781620313640 (hardcover: alk. paper)
ISBN 9781624964114 (ebook)
Subjects: LCSH: Volleyball—Juvenile literature.
Classification: LCC GV1015.34 .D66 2017 (print)
LCC GV1015.34 (ebook) | DDC 796.325—dc23
LC record available at http://lccn.loc.gov/2016007178

Editor: Jenny Fretland VanVoorst
Series Designer: Ellen Huber
Book Designer: Leah Sanders
Photo Researchers: Kirsten Chang, Leah Sanders

Photo Credits: All photos by Shutterstock except:
Getty, 8–9, 10–11; iStock, 4; Thinkstock, 15;
Ververidis Vasilis/Shutterstock.com, 18–19, 23br.

Printed in the United States of America at
Corporate Graphics in North Mankato, Minnesota.

Table of Contents

Let's Play Volleyball!

Grab a ball.

Head to the court.

Let's play volleyball!

Bea's team plays Ana's team. They face each other across the net.

Bea serves.

The ball whizzes over the net.

Ari dives.

He bumps the ball back over the net.

Bea and Beth jump.
They raise their
hands to block.

They miss.

The ball soars past them.

It hits the ground.

Point for Ana's team!

Now Ana serves.

Bea runs to meet the ball.

She bumps it to Brit.

bumping ·····▶

setting

Brit sets the ball.

What happens next?

15

Brian spikes the ball.
Point for Bea's team!

The two teams are tied.

They will play on.

To win, a team must lead by two points.

Do you want to play?
Grab a ball.
Grab some friends.
Volleyball is fun!

On the Volleyball Court

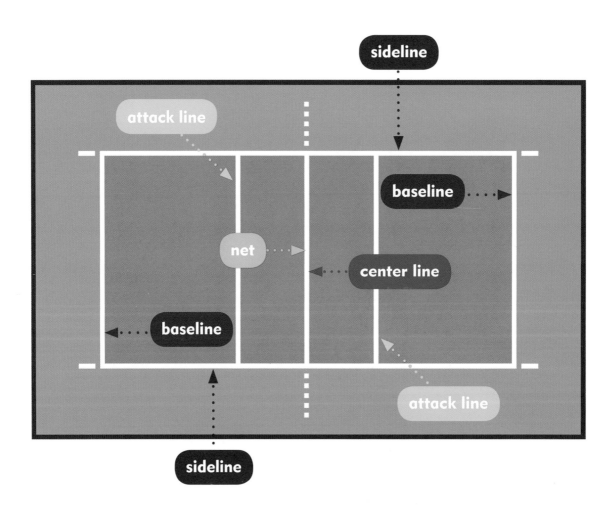

Picture Glossary

bump
A hit designed to pass the ball by getting it up in the air.

spike
A hard downward hit from close to the net.

set
A hit that puts the ball close to the net for a spike.

tied
Having the same score, with neither team ahead or behind.

Index

To Learn More

Learning more is as easy as 1, 2, 3.

1) Go to www.factsurfer.com

2) Enter "volleyball" into the search box.

3) Click the "Surf" button to see a list of websites.

With factsurfer.com, finding more information is just a click away.